AN AUTO

THE RAY BANKS STORY

A TESTIMONY OF GOD'S RESTORATION POWER

Wasteland Press
www.wastelandpress.net
Shelbyville, KY USA

The Ray Banks Story:
A Testimony of God's Restoration Power
by Ray Banks

First Printing – March 2025
Paperback ISBN: 978-1-68111-595-5
Edited by Aqua Robins and Savia Muhammad

Printed in the U.S.A.

0 1 2 3 4

I dedicate this book to every precious soul caught in the matrix of drug addiction who is seeking a way to overcome its stronghold but is unsure how to free themselves. I am someone who was addicted to drugs for years. It is my hope you find confidence in my story. I share this personal journey with you as a door towards your journey to sobriety and peace of mind.

TABLE OF CONTENTS

PREFACE 1

INTRODUCTION 3

CHAPTER ONE: Humble Beginnings 5

CHAPTER TWO: School Days 13

CHAPTER THREE: The Unexpected 19

CHAPTER FOUR: The Slow Unraveling 25

CHAPTER FIVE: A Call to Remembrance 31

CHAPTER SIX: The People and The Places 39

CHAPTER SEVEN: Still Standing 44

CHAPTER EIGHT: Three Decades of Sobriety 48

CHAPTER NINE: Maintenance To Mission 54

CHAPTER TEN: Final Relapse 59

CHAPTER ELEVEN: Extension of Gratitude 67

CHAPTER TWELVE: The Mission of Education 72

CHAPTER THIRTEEN: Deaneen 77

EPILOGUE: The Footsteps of A Trailblazer 88

PREFACE

My purpose for writing this book is to share with the reader the secret to being free of the stronghold of drugs. Sobriety lies in the act of doing what God wants you to do. You might ask yourself, "What does God want me to do?" I will share with you the tried and accurate methods that helped me crush the stronghold of drug addiction, and it will help you, too. This book is life-changing because many drug addicts are seeking sobriety but have nowhere to turn. In this book, you have found the secret door. All you have to do is read the book, trust, and have faith. Try the methods offered, and watch your life change. I want those who suffer from drug addiction to realize that once they recover from drug abuse, their untapped power within will come alive. Drug addictions keep users blinded. These chapters offer real-life solutions to the ever-increasing rate of drug problems growing in America, especially in the black community. This book is my legacy of how I got out of my old life and walked into my new life with the help of God and special people like Dr. John Sullivan, whom you will hear about later in the book. You will read about God-sent men of the church to whom I am indebted because they taught me how to become a man, father, husband, and church leader during the days of my Harvey House ministry. I hope that my life story offers a special message to those addicted to drugs. I hope that the book will inspire those seeking recovery to take sobriety seriously with the perspective that sobriety is a gift to be passed on to others seeking to break through the epidemic of drug addiction.

INTRODUCTION

To be alive to tell my story is nothing short of a miracle. I chose to share every detail of it in hopes someone's faith will increase to know change is possible. I believe anyone who is lost can find their way. Today, I am a man of great hope and a living witness that purpose can emerge from the lowest places in life. The sounds of my life's symphony are not always harmonious but are a beautiful part of my life's song. In the pages of this book is a story of struggle, redemption, love, and grace. It is always rewarding to talk about your accomplishments. However, reciting your harrowing, unfavorable truths not so much. Today, I can rejoice in the distance between my rock-bottom days and a man filled with gratitude for life, family, and the gift of friendship. It is my honor to share my faith and instill hope and support in those who feel hopeless.

CHAPTER ONE
Humble Beginnings

My name is Ray Banks. I was born on September 24, 1959, In Chicago, Illinois. My parents are Preston Willingham and Ruth Banks. I was born the sixth of seven children raised on the west side of Chicago.

My family construct resembled the familiar odds stacked against children being raised in the ghetto of the inner city. Like many others, no father was in our home, only a mother at the helm.

I knew I had a father, but I had only seen him twice since I was born. I truly missed his presence. I somehow understood that it would have been better for me if he had been present.

Due to my father's absence, I questioned if Preston was my father. People often told me I greatly resembled him; however, I couldn't mentally make the connection.

Growing up I can't remember having many positive male figures in my life. My three elder brothers were the males I would take life cues from, and they all learned those cues primarily from the buzz and primitive operations in the streets of Chicago.

Life was difficult for my siblings and me. We had to make do with what my mother could gather for shelter, clothing, and food. Our mother was an uneducated black woman who understood survival and displayed a resilient spirit. She parented out of the struggle of being a single mother raising children among women with a similar fate.

My mother taught me to believe in her words. Once, she told me: "You will be just like your father." That statement embedded itself in my brain, and for years to come, I would somehow prove her right in so many ways.

Ruth and Alice were my elder sisters who left the family house when I was young. I also have three elder brothers, Earl, Carl, and Michael, who lived the ghetto- fabulous way.

I would mimic their behavior by watching them as they joined gangs, sold drugs, and consumed them daily. David was the youngest of the bunch–his examples of greatness, like mine, were non-existent.

It took me years to realize how dysfunctional my upbringing was. Most families around me functioned in the same manner. I honestly thought how we viewed life was functional and acceptable.

I was surrounded by hustlers, crime, sex, violence, and drugs. Interwoven into the fabric of my existence was a culture that welcomed destruction and, in many ways, summoned death. I didn't dream of a better way; I was quite enamored with the life presented to me.

Looking back, I fully embraced the warped philosophy of life instilled in me. I thought a better life was being at the top of the game and nothing else.

Early experiences etched in my memory

At the age of 11, I was left home while my older brothers went to the beach. After they left the house, people with an addiction desiring to buy drugs began to knock on the door. My brother Earl, the ringleader, was selling marijuana at the time.

I was initially irritated by the constant knocking. If you did not know, drug addicts looking for a fix are relentless. After it continued, I figured the only way to stop them from coming was to give them what they wanted. I searched my brother's room and found the drugs. Without a second thought, I began to sell the drugs to the customers.

Oddly, during this impressionable age, I felt no fear. Nothing nagged at my conscience to say, *'Hey Ray, you should not be doing this.'* The business of selling drugs was as natural to me as drinking water. I witnessed what was done, and I simply followed suit.

When my brothers came home, Earl quickly realized his drugs were missing. He confronted me asking where his drugs were. I remember looking at him proudly and saying I sold the drugs. He replied, "You sold the drugs?" I said yes, I sold all of the drugs. That was the day I was officially stamped as a drug dealer.

Reflective Moment: *With my eyes wide open, I realize that an 11-year-old should not live in conditions that expose them to a lifestyle that beckons their demise. Today, I harbor no resentment towards my beautiful mother, absent father, or older siblings. They were all products of the environment and the struggle.*

Being a drug dealer was common where I came from. It was a silent expectation that all the young men in a five-mile radius were fated to experience.

After selling drugs, experimenting with the very drugs you were selling was also very common. Ironically, most dealers who indulged didn't see themselves as addicts; they just enjoyed being high. This disillusionment would be one of the things that aided in the devastation of my life and many others I knew.

My life was fully immersed in the culture of the Westside Ghetto. There were no limits to things that I found myself in. Hustling, drugging, and sexing were considered living the dream, and I was at the top of my game.

Loose living without a care in the world was the norm for most people living in the hood. It was a flashy, nasty, trashy way of life and I for a lengthy time, loved it.

Not having the guidance of a positive male figure caused me to accept life cues from what I saw around me. My sense of self-worth came from an external place. Life was about obtaining things to feel a sense of power. How I appeared to others was far more important than what I felt internally. My feelings were on pause for most of my life.

My little brother's father, Clyde, stayed with us from time to time. He had another family; however, he cheated on his wife with my mother. Being unfaithful was life as I knew it, and I never questioned it. This was another bad trait I picked up along my journey.

I didn't desire to be faithful to a woman. I had not seen it demonstrated and didn't think it was necessary. I had a long list of negative traits, and unfaithfulness was at the top. You will see this play out in another chapter. Keep reading!

I started gambling by shooting dice. Dice was a dangerous game, and when people lost, many fights and threats occurred. I would bet big, win cash, and brag loudly.

One day, Clyde told me that if he caught me shooting dice again, he would put his foot up behind me. I believed him and never let him see me doing that again.

I'm grateful Clyde was present for many things in my life. He showed compassion, which I wasn't used to, but I secretly resented him because he wasn't my father.

Reflective Moment: *As you continue reading, you will hear me mention my absent father often. Writing this book highlighted how much his absence left me wounded. I am forever grateful for every positive male figure that became a part of my journey to health and life. I took this pause to say thank you.*

Whenever I heard anyone talk about their dad it wounded me. I didn't truly know my dad or anyone on his side of the family. I once met a lady with the last name Willingham, and I thought she looked like my dad. I didn't dare to ask her, so that was another opportunity lost to make a connection.

I truly longed for identity. Who am I? Where and what did I indeed come from? These were always looming thoughts, with silent questions always at the forefront.

I only heard bad things about my father. I was often told he did awful things to my mom. My family told me a story about my father coming to our house to fight my mother, and Clyde beat him with an air pump.

Every picture that was painted of him solidified he wasn't good. He was an absent father who abused women. My mom's declaration that I would be just like my father considering this also rings true in my life.

Years after my daughter was born, I looked for my father to tell him I forgave him and to let him see and know I was doing well. It was at this time I discovered through my mother's sister he had died. I was disappointed that I didn't get the chance to speak to him on this side of the grave.

At that moment, I had to embrace the reality that I would never get answers to the many questions I wanted to ask him. I would never know why he made his decisions or know those everyday things about me that reflected him.

CHAPTER TWO
School Days

During my junior high and high school years, living in gang territory became increasingly dangerous. My mother was terrified that I would become hurt if I continued at Manley. She decided that transferring me to Hess Upper Grade Center would be better.

I quickly discovered that there would be no escape from the madness of the streets at Hess Upper-Grade Center. This school fell short of being the "safe place" my mom thought it would be. Drug use and deals were prevalent at the school.

While I attended Hess, my 7th-grade male teacher was not the ideal model for any student, nor did he offer me positive guidance. He was hot-tempered, indulged in drugs, and had an affinity for young boys. He was "totally" inappropriate in his interactions with the students.

I remember him ranting about body odor on three different occasions. He would send all the girls to another class, make the guys line up, and pull down their clothes to find out who had the body odor. We quickly learned that he liked boys, and we tried our best to stay far from his reach.

Sadly, we thought this was horrible, but also, in a way, normal. We were so prone to being amid dysfunction we never thought his behavior was something we should report.

As I think back, the other teachers had to be aware of his behavior. He was flashy in appearance and suggestive in mannerisms. My classmates and I often discussed him while laughing and warning each other not to be alone with him.

This teacher would give three or four of us marijuana, allow us to skip class, and smoke in the coat closet. We would also purchase marijuana for him. Having the green light from the teacher to do drugs made me explore drugs in a greater way. I soon incorporated acid and later heroin into the mix.

I had people that were ready to feed me drugs at any time. The last time I was in the presence of that teacher was to receive my diploma. A group of guys and I went to his classroom to pick up our diplomas. When we entered the classroom, he was overly aggressive that day and made some advances that made us run and escape his grip through the classroom window. As I look back at all that transpired, I am grateful that I wasn't sexually violated.

Years after leaving Hess, an old classmate of mine was sent to prison for murdering that teacher. I never knew the details of what happened, but in the back of my mind, I felt he murdered the teacher dealing with something that started in high school and was never spoken of openly. The teacher's murder is what I meant when I said life around me seemed to summon death.

Strangely, despite all the issues and negative experiences mounting in my life, I was a fast learner. In preparation for high school, I missed opportunities to attend Lane Tech, Jones Commercial, and Lindblom, known for their academic and athletic success.

Those schools would provide a different academic experience and an opportunity to dream. I remember being so excited about the opportunity, but when I shared it with my mother, she did not share my enthusiasm.

Due to my mom's lack of encouragement, I didn't take the test, and the subject wasn't mentioned again. When school started in the fall of September, I was enrolled in a neighborhood school with all the guys I grew up with, and life continued as usual.

The oppressive atmosphere I came from suffocated people. No one dreamed or envisioned their way out of the hood. People became comfortable and found themselves in daily survival mode. You did not often find anyone looking towards the future; they were busy trying to get through the day. Many opportunities passed me by, I settled into life as I knew it and became cozy with all that came with it.

Thinking outside the scope of your everyday experiences and those experienced by your peers' struggles was unspoken. If any part of the struggle of life was beneath you, and you voiced it, you were ridiculed for thinking you were better than others.

I enrolled in Austin High School with many of my neighborhood buddies. As you might imagine, it was another bad decision. My friends and I spent more time outside of school than inside.

The Lincoln Park Zoo was free, so we gravitated to it. There, we would get high, chase girls, and talk smack. We were also fascinated by the animals.

I had two great friends, Half Piece and J-Boogie, and when you saw me, you would see them. We were a group of misfits, but we cared deeply for one another. If something outrageous happened, we were right there in the thick of it.

In the middle of the school year, I decided to go to school and play football. However, an employment opportunity was offered. I like money, so I decided to take the job. At this time, I wasn't making a lot of money selling drugs, so taking the job was the priority.

Having money afforded me the chance to stand out from the rest of the crowd. My mother was a public aid recipient with seven children. Mama had no fancy clothing and shoes in her budget. In her house, we ate government food in white boxes, wore hand-me-down clothing, and slept in small quarters.

The saying "When you look good, you feel good" is true. It felt good to buy nice things, and throughout most of my life, I maintained a legitimate source of income alongside my street hustle.

CHAPTER THREE
The Unexpected

Some things happen that seemingly snatch the air out of your lungs. Those things that you never imagined you would find yourself standing in.

Death, dope, and devastation are things I was well acquainted with. I didn't think much of it, because it was the way of life. Even with that, reality never prepares you when it hits the ones you love the most.

My brother Carl's girlfriend, Blanche, gave him a ring. I stole it from him and got it stuck on my finger. Carl was so upset about the ring that he took my favorite necklace with the cross charm as his vindication.

Carl was my big brother so demanding it back would not prove to be an intelligent request. I would have to wade through it and continue trying to figure out how to get the ring off my finger and return it.

One day, he approached me, returned the necklace, and told me he wanted his ring. I tried to return the ring, but it was seemingly attached to my finger.

Not many days after that conversation, I received word my older brother Carl had been shot.

Earl yelled the news out to me while running past the housing projects toward Mt. Saini Hospital, the hospital Carl was taken to by ambulance and pronounced dead.

I can't remember what took place between me learning Carl was shot and me making it to the hospital; it seems that time stood still. I remember sitting in the hospital next to Mama telling her all would be well. Seconds later, a doctor and detective came to tell us he hadn't made it.

The doctor informed us that his lungs filled with blood, and he was unable to breathe. He had one gunshot to the chest, and just like that he was gone. I sat holding my inconsolable mother. I couldn't hold back the tears, nor could my older brother Earl, we were all in the deep trenches of pain.

At Carl's funeral, I sat there playing with his ring that was stuck on my finger. On this day, it loosened and slid off my finger. I walked up to the casket and put the ring on his finger. He had finally got his ring back.

Reflective Moment: *This entire ring story is quite mysterious. Something you often attempt and fail to do happens momentarily, reminding you that all is not always lost. Putting that ring on his finger brought me a bit of peace. He loved it, and I was finally able to return it.*

Carl's death affected my mom in ways I can't fully explain. She stopped enforcing rules and allowed us to sell drugs and smoke marijuana in the house. She lived in quiet fear. The pain of losing her child rested with her in ways I can't describe. She became somewhat subdued; she was happy to know her other sons were alive.

After the death of my brother, I was smoking marijuana, selling and digesting drugs more frequently. The hustle became increasingly dangerous. I was in the grips of grief and addiction; sensible fear was not a thing.

Our hood at this time was on the radar of law enforcement. We were increasingly experiencing turf wars that included armed robberies and deaths. I felt no pressure to get out of the lifestyle. I found new and devious ways to continue my craft and didn't think much of the matter.

One day, while sitting in J-Boogie's house, known as the "spot," my brother Earl, who was highly connected to the streets, stopped by to pick up drugs. He was disgusted by my presence and scolded me in front of everyone. He called me a nobody! He was living the same life but was disgusted that I had gotten caught up. This encounter deeply wounded me; his opinion cut like a knife.

Thinking back, I know he wanted something different for me. I no longer resembled the brother he once knew. He had already lost one brother, and I could have easily become next.

As drug trafficking and consumption increased, I would hear of people overdosing, going to jail, and getting beaten in the streets. It was the way of life as I knew it. I would acknowledge what was happening and continue in my disillusionment.

Things were spiraling out of control. My good friends Half Piece, Jay Boogie, and my ex-girlfriend Anna went to jail for selling drugs. These were my sidekicks and the closest people to me at the time. I was devastated because, for me, it was like losing family members. I was also thankful that I escaped jail.

We found creative ways to try and conceal our hustle. I remember wrapping marijuana in the newspaper around the inside of my hat to appear unassuming to law enforcement and robbers. Nothing was off-limits for me. Stashing drugs in baby bassinets, refrigerators, and in places under clothing that I let you imagine and will not voice.

I became increasingly cunning and increasingly bold in my embrace of street life. I was living free from any responsibility or accountability, and more unexpected things were on the horizon.

I was amid one transition after another at this time, including the loss of my brother and my friends, exploring new drugs, and moving out from one section of the West side to another.

Everything around me was changing rapidly. Becoming the person of power in the street was shifting how once friends and family related to each other—the decline in people you could trust increased in my world. I often lived in a state of paranoia and looking over my shoulder was a common practice.

Drugs were calling and I was answering. No one was exempt from being double-crossed, manipulated, and lied to. The saying: *"birds of feathers flock together"* is for sure. People with addictions hung around drug addicts, and that meant cutthroat action happened regularly.

CHAPTER FOUR
The Slow Unraveling

I met Izola, who I affectionately named Dimples. I had a fling with Izola, but I was not faithful. I had never seen men show genuine care for women. I was no different than any other male I knew. I used women for my pleasure and wanted nothing more than that.

I started watching pornography around the age of 15. This opened my world to a sexual obsession. I made it a quest to sleep with as many women as possible. It also was a known fact that drugs were an enhancement to sex. I wanted sex and drugs, so the combination was my fascination.

I moved from one part of the city to another and had not seen Izola in about ten months. A guy from the neighborhood informed me that Izola had a little girl who was my baby. I wasn't sure about this, yet it would prove to be another transition in my life: fatherhood.

Fatherhood, wow! I had no reference for this transition. I did not have a father in my life. I did not know how to feel about this possibility. What I could offer was a silent but looming question ruminating in my mind.

The first time I met my baby girl, Charla, I ran into Izola on the streets. I asked her whether the rumors about her being my daughter were true. She confirmed that I was the father of the child.

It wasn't unusual for girls from the hood to get pregnant and never tell their father about the child. Most girls knew the guys wouldn't pursue a relationship with the child, especially if they were no longer spending time with the guy. The one thing I loathed was my absentee father; for a short time, I once again proved to be like mine.

This new reality did not change me, but it awakened me somehow. Izola and I were in a trusting relationship when Charla was two years old. Charla was a beautiful girl who loved to ask questions. She once asked why buildings in the neighborhood were called Court Way buildings. I still don't know the answer to that question, laughing out loud. I told her it was because it was a shared entryway into the various units.

Izola and I moved into an apartment over a bar owned by my aunt. During this time, me and my family were smoking crack heavily. Having crack addicts as family members all living in one place proved to be at the height of crazy. We would get high together, steal from each other, and fight like sworn enemies.

Izola, my new wife, was now living amid madness. She was pregnant and having our children. I was so detached from what she was feeling. My entire world revolved around drugs, and sadly she and neither were the children a priority.

Reflective Moment: *When my first daughter Charla was born, I was addicted. When Racheal, Pamela, and my son Freddie were born, I was heavily addicted. Later, you will read of the redemptive work and the resurrection to the correct position in fatherhood. For this, I am most thankful. I will also* *take this moment to offer an apology to Izola on these pages for the world to see.*

Living in my aunt's building was no longer a safe space. The danger we faced led us to move to her mother's basement. In Izola's mother's basement, I continued to sell and take drugs. I had savings through various entities from my jobs, making it easier to get high. I had money coming in continuously.

Drug dealers knew I would have their money, so they started giving me drugs even when I had no cash on hand. The crack habit led to all sorts of chaos. In this season of my life crack was all I could think about.

I sold drugs to get high. I would party, work a legitimate job, occasionally sleep, and repeat that format daily. The crack addiction was getting crazier at this time. Taking long trips while standing in one spot was the norm. I would get so high that I would have no memory of what happened the day before.

I had different types of pipes: Little Bertha, Big Bertha, and Show Gun. I would set them all out and smoke them in different order. I was living on cloud nine and often joked about going on the Tonight Show to share that I had found a new heaven.

At this crazy time in my life, Izola and I managed to buy the 4-unit building from her aunt. I was now collecting rent for three units. For a while, I could save money and invest in savings bonds. I didn't think I was so bad off. I just knew I was living the life.

I talked about getting a second property and becoming a real estate agent. Around this time, I had progressed in my crack consumption, and my dream of becoming a real estate agent was just an illusion. My ability to hold on to a legitimate job had become unmanageable. At this point, I came face to face with the reality that I needed help. I was in a bad way. I started robbing and stealing to feed my addiction.

Once, a couple of friends and I attempted to rob a drunk guy. Luckily, for the guy, the police came before we could complete the task. However, later that day we robbed a guy at gunpoint and took his money. He only had $37 and a check we couldn't cash.

Plagued by the thought of possibly killing the guy, this incident made me want to rethink my life. I was living in a state of delusion. I still wasn't convinced that I was addicted. I attempted to convince myself that I just needed to get away for a while and clear my mind. This was the first decision I made to seek out a treatment center.

CHAPTER FIVE
A Call to Remembrance

I checked myself in at Loretto Hospital Rehabilitation Center on the city's west side, with no long-term relief plan. It was there that I accepted the label of being an addict.

The counselor introduced me to the Bible and told me God loves me. He also told me to read Matthew 6:33, which states, *"Seek ye first the Kingdom of God and his righteousness."* This scripture was the first scripture I read, and it stayed in my mind, but I wasn't ready to take heed.

I stayed long enough to rest up. As soon as I was released, I went to the neighborhood to score drugs. Smoking crack was my passion, there was no greater feeling in the world at that time in my life.

I have so many shameful stories I can share. Being an addict stripped me of my dignity, and it assisted in my no-limits way of living. Whatever it took to cure my drug ache was a thing.

I remember going to a girl's house who was living in a condemned building. She was there with a few other people, a place where people with addictions gathered to buy and consume drugs. The police came to raid the house and I told her to wrap the 10-15 bags of drugs in her hair. We purposefully left residue on the mirror so the police could focus on that. When the police left, we smoked the remainder of the drugs.

I wasn't sure if I was hallucinating or understood that the other addicts were setting me up. I suddenly panicked and knew I needed to leave. I conveniently told them I had more dope in another apartment and would come right back. I never came back; I escaped again.

Reflective Moment: *I could have died several times in my life. I could also have been imprisoned for long periods. None of these experiences were an opposing match for addiction. All* *the lies I told myself couldn't cover how low I stooped down to get high.*

Once, I smoked in my female cousin's house. She claimed to have no money for drugs. After getting high on my drugs, she suddenly produced $40 to go buy drugs. I remember being angry that she had lied about having money. I agreed to go and get more drugs. I swindled her this time and never went back to her house. I got the drugs and smoked them without her.

Embedded deep in my mind is a story I am about to share with you. I knew I was in over my head when I visited my dear mother and lied about being in danger. I told her people were outside waiting for me and would come into her house if she didn't give me money. She initially said no, but I pleaded with her until she gave in. I can remember her reluctance and her solemn expression. The worst part is, at the time, not even my sweet mother was off-limit when I was chasing a high.

Hurting people that love me most, despite their love and devotion for me, was not a consideration. The most effortless punch is directed at the people closest to you. It is a blessed thing that the people you love love you so much that they choose not to abuse or kill you.

As I continued to reflect on some of the lowest moments in my life, I am thankful to God that I made it through those days. I stayed for long periods in abandoned buildings and apartments with addicts. My wife and children would not see me for days on in.

One day, while in the crack house, someone came to tell me my wife was in labor. I was so caught up in the addiction I disregarded what anyone had to say and continued to get high.

I can't remember how many hours it took me to get to the hospital. During that time, I got robbed and high at the same time. I could not assist Izola because I was tweaking. I was so far out of my head that I couldn't tell if I was coming or going.

When I finally exited the high, I visited my furious wife. That night, I stayed overnight reluctantly. My wife was in the same room as she was the previous year when she gave birth to my daughter, Racheal.

When I first saw my infant daughter, Pamela, I knew she would be a blessing. She gave me a look of love that resonated with me. Her love and loyalty as my daughter remain true even now. She is always by my side.

I realized now that I needed long-term help and decided to go back to the rehab center at Loretto Hospital. During the birth of my daughter, I realized that using drugs was wrong. I regularly went to the rehab center for treatments, and although I was more open to receiving and accepting, I was no match for the addiction. I still wasn't fully ready to live without crack cocaine.

* * *

I was delusional and lived so far from reality. I was back in the thick of it all. One day I was in an abandoned building with my cousin, and someone tried to kill us. Addicts needed to get high, and robberies were happening frequently. This reflection brings tears to my eyes. I escaped again. That should have gotten my attention, but it didn't.

Once you start smoking cocaine, there is nothing on earth that is more important. While in the madness of addiction, the drive and hustle to always indulge takes you to unimaginable places.

I was looking to score drugs, and a homosexual who lived in the area was prancing and dancing around flamboyantly. My first thought was, "I can get money from him." I approached him and went into his house. I allowed him to give me a blow job. This sexual act was a new low, and I was immediately overtaken by shame. As a heterosexual male, this should have been non-negotiable.

After this encounter, I was so devastated at what I had become that I left and didn't even take the man's money. I remember riding around seeing that guy years later and experiencing a sinking feeling in the pit of my stomach of how low I went. I am sure the guy didn't even remember me. I was just another conquest in the world of addiction.

I have so many horror stories connected to the life of a drug addict. They are painful to reflect upon. I didn't think of how my destructive behavior was impacting others. I can genuinely say I know what it feels like to be lost.

I once stayed at my sister Alice's house to look after her kids. I found a gun that looked weird. After picking up the gun, I decided to pull the trigger. The bullet hit the couch and caused a fire. I quickly put the fire out and hid the hole by pushing the sofa against the wall.

I was constantly tweaking and not thinking of the consequences. That day could have ended in a greater tragedy. It could have been the death of a person and not just a couch or possibly a house.

I once gave my daughter Charla $20 for her birthday. I dropped her off at school and asked her to let me borrow the money, which I would give back later. Daily, I was topping the last low with a new one. When I returned my daughter's birthday money, I showed her another example of fatherhood gone wild.

My wife, Izola, had accepted that if I didn't find long-term help, I would be in the grave soon. She somehow found a police officer who connected her to an alderman who told her about a 6-month program at Brandon House.

My wife was pregnant with our first son, Freddie. By this time, my drugged-out lifestyle dragged her down so much that she told me she was moving to Milwaukee with our three kids. I didn't think she would do it, but she did, and Freddie was born there.

CHAPTER SIX
The People and The Places

It took a great deal of time for me to partner up with the reality that I could have a more fantastic future. Rehab wasn't working for me, because I wasn't willing to do the work.

During my first trip to Brandon House, I accepted Jesus Christ. White people were trying to lead me to the Lord. At that time, I was so prejudiced against white people that it was hard to receive from them. I was at this time more convinced that I needed a Savior, I just didn't think a Caucasian was the right person to help me.

I went to a black church, and honestly, accepting the Lord in that atmosphere felt better. Reverend Alexander Barnes led me to the Lord. I kept going to Bible study with white people coming to the center, and I was just happy to break the routine of the day-to-day life there.

Barbara Sullivan, a white woman passionate about the Lord, taught me about Jesus Christ. She awakened in me a hunger to know the Lord better. I became so committed to God that I began to apply what I was learning to my life. I decided to follow what the Bible said about sinning (my drug use) rather than my previous environment.

When I became the program's house elder, I knew I could make it. God had redeemed me, and I enjoyed helping others grow in their faith and assisting them in navigating their road to recovery. Things were good for a while. When I was discharged, I would love to say I stayed clean.

I moved back in with my mother. Two weeks after I moved in, all my buddies from the projects came to see me. They had drugs: weed, cocaine, heroin, and happy sticks.

They laid all the drugs on the table, and I told them I didn’t get high anymore and I didn’t want the drugs. I thanked them for thinking of me, but God had set me free. They left disgusted and in disbelief that I would say that. I convinced myself I was done with drugs. I wanted to be free.

I went back to work, and things were going well. My wife and I were shopping for a new place to stay. Three or four weeks after rehab, I met up with this female, and I was trying to have sex with her, but she was trying to get crack. Sex was on the table along with crack. Together, we indulged in crack, which took the fight out of me to resist sex.

I was smoking crack once again; it became my refuge, and I couldn't stop. I thought this was my lot in life. I started calling Greg Robinson, who became my counselor and friend. When he would answer, I would just hang up. He was a person that didn't cut corners. I nick-named him "Human Hemorrhoid."

When I smoked crack, I found myself misusing people for money. One day, I was with a cousin who was selling crack out of an abandoned building, and eventually, that was where I lived. I lived there for six or seven days a week. When I smoked crack, it tore me from the floor up, which is a disgusting version of a human being.

On the weekend of my birthday, I smoked cocaine for days. I had money coming in from various places. I was selling dope out of a place we called the murder building. Some people enter to rob us. A girl had sprayed something that made me delirious. I told the guys I had more cocaine, and this enabled me to get away.

That night I walked a long way to get to my house. Once I reached the crib, I grabbed my cocaine stash and went to a girl's house and smoked cocaine all night. At one point, I took off my shoes to lie down. I went without bathing until my socks stuck to my feet. The reality of this devastated me.

The next day, I called Brandon House to check in for the second time. I was going back to rehab for the fourth time. I was there washing my clothes and my friend showed up with drugs. We did the drugs, and they wanted to get more, but for some reason, I didn't go with them. I now attribute this to the Holy Spirit. I had a ride to the rehab center. I packed my clothes while still wet, and I made it there.

I was back at Brandon House, and before I knew it, they called my name to sign into the program. I already knew Manny Gonzalez, a fantastic counselor who always supported me and I needed to hear what the people from Spirit of God Fellowship would offer me. I went through the program quickly, with only a few run ends.

I attended the Spirit of God Fellowship on Wednesdays during the resident visit to Brandon House. There, I met Pastor Dr. John Sullivan. I liked attending church on Wednesdays because it temporarily allowed me to escape the four walls of Brandon House.

In this place, I was set free from sexual, drug, and cigarette addiction. I had become, in my mind, a leader in Christ. I knew, somehow, I was going to make it.

They began talking about a place called the Restoration Ministry/Harvey House. It was somewhere I needed to be. Harvey House is where I am today, and I have many stories from it. It was the beginning of a new life in Christ. Although it was a six-month resident program, I planned to stay for 30 days. I have been there now for 35 years.

CHAPTER SEVEN
Still Standing

In 1991, I became a Youth Pastor for Restoration Ministries. Little did I know that this calling on my life would mark the beginning of a magnificent youth program for local school-aged children.

My first assignment with the youth came at the request of Mrs. Mabel Young, the Building Principal at Gwendolyn Brooks Middle School. She said she was having a gang problem and told me she heard I was working with the kids in the neighborhood. She asked me to visit the school to minister to the kids, and I accepted her invitation.

After listening to and observing the students, I realized the school had no gang problem. They were students who wanted to be associated with a gang.

Once we ironed out that small challenge at Gwendolyn Brooks Middle School, everything, including the students, was okay.

The same year, Restoration Ministries partnered with Silver Birch Ranch, a camping site for families and children in White Lake, Wisconsin, six hours away from Chicago. We started taking kids to camp, including boys and girls, so they could see the positive side of life and have something to look forward to during Spring breaks and summer. The camp visit was a seven-day stay during which students learned so much.

The children could go to the camp through the Silver Birch Ranch Scholarship Foundation, which was an all-paid trip for each child who attended. During their camp experience, students had access to horse riding, jet skiing, water, and snow tubing.

For many years, during the summer, we have sent 100 junior high school students to Silver Birch Ranch in Wisconsin. We also started taking kids to the Young Life Camp in North Carolina, Minnesota, New York, and Michigan.

The partnership between Silver Birch and Restoration Ministries is still intact today, thanks to my daughter,

Pamela, who, since 2014, has served as Manager of Youth Program for Restoration Ministries. When she was young, my daughter worked with the youth programs as far back as when I first started Youth Ministries programs.

1994, I also visited Thornridge, Thornton, and Thornwood High Schools to discuss my youth group program.

In 1996, ten years into recovery, my daughter Charla was a sophomore in high school. One morning, I asked Charla what she remembered most about my addiction. She said I never paid the $20 back I gave her for her birthday. I was devastated after hearing that.

Later that day, I picked her up from school and returned the $20. We sat in the parking lot laughing and crying. She proceeded to tell me many stories. This, for me, was the ugly of it; my children knew and witnessed the brokenness of my drug addiction. Charla, being the oldest, had seen it all. After listening to her, I realized she was acutely aware that I was *once* a bonafide addict. Telling my ugly stories stopped my children and many of their friends from using drugs.

As I put the past behind me, little by little, my life started to take a turn for the better. I started noticing the change in my attitude and how I looked at things. I no longer thought about drugs or desired to be around drugs. By now, my compassion to help people to heal themselves from drug use was in the whole operation. I wanted more for myself during this time, but I wasn't sure how those things would come about. I kept believing it would. As time passed, everything was looking good. The thought of owning a home stayed on my mind, and I wanted to purchase a house to take care of my family. It was what real men and birth fathers do.

It was time for the things that meant something to me to start showing up in my life, like owning a new home and having my family in one place.

The new home would be the beginning of the many blessings I received. God showed me that if I trusted in him during the many dark days, hours, and years of drug addiction, he would walk by my side and bless me. The Bible says that when you have done all you can, continue to stand, and I did. I don't regret waiting on God for my deliverance and blessings. I'm still standing because of God's favor in my life.

CHAPTER EIGHT
Three Decades of Sobriety

Dr. Sullivan, the Pastor of SOGF, invited me to his home to study the Bible. I declined the invitation because we had already learned enough at the Harvey House. He asked me multiple times, and I finally went.

I was the only black guy in the room, and we talked about the disciples while we were there. Dr. Sullivan asked prayer for upcoming trips to Africa, Mexico, and Jamaica to start church plants and businesses. I finally spoke up to say I wanted to travel to Jamaica with him.

My ex-wife worked for the airline, allowing me to sit in first class while Dr. Sullivan sat in the coach section. When I got to Jamaica, they treated me like a celebrity, which Dr.

Sullivan found entertaining. Once we landed in Jamaica, I met many people who were part of the straw market. I remember evangelizing with them down a long alleyway. I also met Denton and Anthony, the Jamaican contacts who assisted Harvey House with our ministry while we were there.

Sometimes, I stayed in Jamaica for more than two months. I started taking men from the Harvey House who were recovering with us. During that time, Jamaica became a second home for me, and again, the new man in me continued to emerge, as Dr. Sullivan had foreseen many years before our missionary work in Jamaica. I remembered how Dr. Sullivan would fly in with a team of dentists offering free dental services throughout Jamaica.

The level of kindness and servitude I witnessed as I journeyed with Dr. Sulllivan impacted me personally. His service to others made me a better human. We bought soccer shoes for all the kids in the hills and ministered Christ to them. Giving back to the Jamaican soccer team was Dr. Sullivan's love language, and everyone who knew him benefitted. As I journeyed with Dr. Sullivan, my life and cultural experiences expanded.

After the soccer game, we gave out shirts, and I requested that they let us wash them. The soccer team refused and left, returning to the hills. I was mad about this and decided to go to the mountains to confront them. To my surprise, they were waiting to confront me.

I learned so much that day, and it was humbling. I submitted to learning from them, and while I was in Jamaica, I learned much about the food, culture, and language. I realized I was there to gain knowledge and insight into the culture and people to become an attentive teacher.

Dr. Sullivan became a great mentor and friend. He would tell me to stick with him. He was like the dad I never had. He once said, "Stick with me, and you will be able to preach to those on 45th under the El station and near Prestwick Park." He said I would minister in the ghetto and the suburbs.

While on an outing, Dr. Sullivan told me I would run for the school board. I came to Harvey House to learn to become a minister, so the school board was off my radar. I shared a list of reasons why I should not be on the board. He said, "Forget about that and run. If you don't win, oh well."

I ran for the school board seat and got more votes than any other candidate. It was the dawning of a new day for me. As Dr. Sullivan had predicted, my future would again outweigh my past, and a new man in me would emerge.

I implemented many things that directly impacted the school district's student body. Dr. Sullivan's quote came into my head. He said, "I heard a lot about your past, but I am excited about your future." Under his guidance, I would become a youth pastor, elder, and executive director of Restoration Ministries. He would have me work outside my comfort zone by preparing for a future I couldn't have imagined.

My ex-wife planned on moving to Schaumburg, Illinois, with the kids, but I didn't want her to. They were set to leave in five days. During a Thursday morning meeting, I spoke to Dr. Sullivan about my situation with my ex-wife, who was moving the kids to Schaumburg, and I wasn't happy about it. I saw a house I already liked, and immediately, he stopped the meeting and suggested we go and take a look at it. He wanted the house and asked if I had money to put down. I only had a thousand dollars to put down.

The blessing to purchase my first home came about when Dr. Sullivan and other board members asked me to be the executive director of Restoration Ministries. I got the position that came with a $20K bonus. My ex-wife let the children stay with me, even though I had no credit established to get the house. Two years prior, I asked my ex-wife to give me the mortgage payment, and this would become a line of credit, and tithing would become my second line of credit. God used this to open the door for home ownership.

Charla asked about the house, and I told her I had gotten it. The entire family erupted with applause, and we, yes "we," were ready to move in. We had no furniture, but God's favor for me was all around. Someone even suggested I have a housewarming party. Dr. Sullivan announced I got the house during church service but needed more rooms. All the plumbers and electricians in the church fully remodeled the basement to add three bedrooms, a living room, and a bathroom. After that came a lovely housewarming celebration.

My life took on new meaning. Blessings and opportunities kept showing up in my life. God was working on my behalf. I knew all these things weren't happening because I put them into action; they were happening because God had His hand on my life.

CHAPTER NINE
Maintenance To Mission

Witnessing and counseling drug addicts is how I became a minister, although I knew nothing about being a minister with no former seminary training. Deep down, all I wanted to do was free myself of drugs and get close to my kids again.

The rehab program had a calling in my life: to serve as a minister. The idea of becoming a minister pulled and tugged on me, and I could not and would not resist the calling to go forth. The first thing I heard in my spirit about becoming a minister was, *"Seek ye first the kingdom of God, and all things will be added unto thee."* I can't say my walk was perfect because no one starts in ministry knowing everything or doing everything right. Still, I was willing to answer God's call.

The Harvey House program offered me a new level of sobriety. I became committed by attending church service whenever the doors opened, and I figured I could help others since several of Dr. Sullivan's rehab programs helped me.

The church was strong in giving back, and I wanted to do what it was doing because, in my heart, it was the right thing to do. At this point, I had many positive examples of church leaders before me, and my life was remarkably better.

As I learned new things about drug addiction in bible study and through becoming a minister, I felt compelled to reach out and lift others who were at their lowest. I thought about the lows I was in for years. I know how I felt floundering in the mud of addiction. I wanted to set people free. Jesus did it, and I knew I could do it too.

Everything I learned about drug addiction, I taught it to other people struggling with drugs, those who were trying to get out of the vicious cycle of drug abuse. I had no formal training on the subject of addiction, yet I was willing to teach addicts anything I knew. The Harvey House gave me the boost to effectively teach addicts to get back on their feet after falling to rock bottom levels.

In Christianity, there is a saying that it's better to give than to receive, and I gave valuable information on drug addiction. Whether I talked about forgiveness or addiction, I would freely share the message with those who needed to hear it.

I overcame my issues by listening to the instructions and stories that others shared with me, and I was blessed with their help and guidance to get through my drug problem.

Remember, I questioned God about Him sending Mexicans and whites to teach me to overcome my addiction, even though the Spirit of God Fellowship Church I attended was ninety percent white, eight percent black, and two percent Mexican.

Years later, I understood how influential these multiracial leaders were and why they were in my life.

God ordained these men from other races to deliver me from drug use to heal, restore, and prepare me for several ministries I didn't see coming. I didn't know God was taking me somewhere to help other people of all races and backgrounds. Because I was in such a dark, dismal place ten years before deliverance, my destiny was one I couldn't envision nor see coming to fruition.

I also realized that the outcome of my healing and deliverance of drug addiction outweighed the gross misunderstanding of why those leaders were there in the first place.

You see, both white and Mexican leaders for the church's drug program carried a message from God to me. Addictions touch all races. Through his grace, God transmits divine messages of hope, healing, deliverance, and restoration through people of all races, no matter their color, to heal us with any problems we face. Recognizing this was a sobering revelation for me.

Even while using drugs heavily, I knew I desperately needed deliverance, but I did not know when or how it was going to happen. God never shows us everything at once about the outcome of our lives or how we will get out of a bad situation. He wants us to have the patience and faith to overcome our adversities.

Also, in all his wisdom, God will send anyone to help us in our situations. He will send people in many disguises to rescue us, whether black, white, or brown. God's Will causes people to assist us in times of need. So, we must trust what God does for us and know that he won't leave nor forsake us. We must have a willing mind and heart to know God is calling us to come out of our addictions.

Little did I know, the remarkable things about drug addiction I learned through the Harvey House program would dramatically change my life forever. God is at the center of our lives. We must trust him and be willing to take the next step toward change, and that's what I did. You can do it too!

Not only was I able to help myself overcome some of the most challenging addictions anyone can suffer from, but with the spiritual guidance of God, the Spirit of God Fellowship Church, Harvey House, Brandon House, and Restoration Ministries, I was successful in bridging the gap between addiction and sobriety; helping people of all races to throw away the pipe, the pill, and the powder. In doing so, this is how God changed my drug rehab journey from maintenance to mission.

CHAPTER TEN
Final Relapse

In rehab, they told me that drug addiction works congruently with other addictions. Let me tell you how this is possible. I was about twelve years old when I started having sex, which was the beginning of my sexual addiction. The first girl I got involved with was a few years older than me, so to get next to her, I lied about my age, and before I knew it, I was sexually involved with an older teenager. Smoking marijuana was easy access, because my brother sold weed right from our house. Follow me through this looping journey.

After using marijuana for a while, I started using heroin, PCP, and cocaine. I eventually stopped using them, but what didn't stop was this insatiable, unexplainable need for sex. I wasn't aware that I had a sexual addiction until many years later while in rehab.

The prostitutes I spent time with during those years were after the drugs, and I was after the sex. I gave them money and drugs, and they gave me what I wanted, and that was sex. So, now I'm all mixed up with sex and drugs, only to learn later both are an evil mix against the brain.

One thing I noticed about my sexual addiction pattern was that I only wanted to have sex when I was using drugs. Drugs serve as a sexual enhancement that puts you on a high, and they also increase the pleasure of sexual intimacy and endurance.

My ah-ha moment concerning my sexual addiction problem came one evening in a rehab session when I openly and candidly spoke about the timing of using drugs, which happened just before sex. Everyone in that rehab session's eyes lit up and agreed that my statement was true.

It's a scientific fact that there's a small portion of the brain that controls both sexual and drug addictions called the basal ganglia, which controls sexual pleasure, habits, and routines. The saving grace for this condition is that once a person gets past the sexual addiction, he can overcome the drug addiction.

My last and final relapse happened during a time when I was in the process of trying to overcome my drug addiction. Remember, it was later on that I discovered the silent but loud sexual addiction. I have a story to share about my last encounter with this monster.

I went to the west side one day after church to drop a church member off. He had moved back in with his mother to the west side, and he asked me if I could take him home, and I did.

After dropping him off at his mom's, the next series of events became a slippery slope for me. On that fateful Wednesday evening, unknowing to me, I was wide open for stuff I knew wasn't good for me, period. All my rehab guards and protective mechanisms that I learned lowered to ground zero, and the evil force of sex and drugs had gathered force. I didn't take a staff person from the church with me who could have easily intercepted the events that happened to me that night.

I didn't realize my vulnerability until after it was all over. God will test you on those things you love the most to bring to bear a dark side of yourself in exchange for healing.

After I dropped off my friend, the devil in my head went to work, and I went along with the propositions that the devil offered me. I went looking for a woman in the streets and found her. She was someone that I didn't know, and after being introduced, we got together and had sex, and during that time, drugs came into play.

I used drugs starting that Wednesday night with that girl and stayed with her until Friday morning, two days later. After leaving the westside, I headed back to the south suburbs. My car broke down on 79th Street, and I caught the bus to a Southside motel, and I continued to do drugs after checking in.

With nowhere to go except to stay in my room, I got up enough nerves to call Manny Gonzalez, director of the Harvey House Program. I told him about my lost weekend and wild escapade with this girl I had met. Instead of being down on me, Manny gave me strict instructions not to go anywhere and said that in 25 minutes, he and Tony Salerno, another employee at Harvey House, would come to pick me up. Thirty minutes later, I arrived at Harvey House, where I had started my ministry.

Relapses like this happen every day; nothing new, right? You know, people with an addiction get caught up when they don't see how one addiction triggers the other. It happens when we aren't aware that hidden addictions are activated when other addictions are present. I thought I was fighting drugs, but the real problem was the hidden sex addiction, ignited by the drug habit and vice-versa. It is indeed a vicious cycle.

The truth is, after all of that two-day involvement with sex and drugs, I thought it was over as far as being a minister. I let two days of madness ruin my life. I thought they were through with me for sure. When I returned to the ministry days later from my lost weekend, there was no mention of being expelled from Harvey House. The opposite happened. After arriving at Harvey House, where I lived, Manny quietly said, "Hey Ray, go upstairs and get ready; we're going on a men's retreat this weekend to learn about God," that was all that was said. If that wasn't God working on my behalf, I don't know what it was.

During Harvey House training, I never previously had deliverance from sexual addictions. Months later, after the last sexual encounter I had with the girl on the west side, a spiritual revelation helped me to see that I had a sexual addiction. Although I realized having a sexual conquest with a stranger was risky. When the dust settled, and I stood back up on both feet, that experience helped me to see that drugs were my problem, but my sexual addiction was the center core of my problem. Once I overcame my sex addiction, I had no more problems with drugs or anything.

I had to change some things around to help my sexual addiction. No longer did I view women as an object to have sex with, which was taught to me as a young boy. The unknown female who I had sex with was a blessing to me; even though what Satan meant for evil, God turned it around for good. That final relapse experience with that girl helped me to see the sexual addiction that had blinded me.

If God hadn't prompted me to call Manny Gonzalez while I was at that motel by myself on 79th Street and let him know how I had messed up and that I was using again, I would have died of a drug overdose or locked up in jail. Over those two days of using, I headed back to a life of lunacy because I was constantly looking for drugs, and I didn't care about life or who I hurt.

Relapse happens, and when it does, consider doing the following things to help you move forward to a happier and more peaceful life:

1. **Surround yourself with new friends**

The old friends are about themselves and drugs. The new friends you meet are about sobriety and living a clean lifestyle. They don't visit the past just to relapse.

2. **Be honest with yourself about your drug or sex habits.**

Admitting to the addiction is the first step toward healing. Getting help to stop the addictions is the next step. The first step of a thousand miles begins with that first step. Seek out holistic drug programs that treat the mind and the body. Attend spiritual retreats that promote overcoming addictions and offer healing and deliverance.

3. Curve your sexual appetite.

Sex is a powerful, natural force, and when it goes unchecked, it can become anybody's worst nightmare. To overcome your sexual addiction, think about how you view women and women and how you view men. Yes, women also have sexual addictions too. As for the men, when you realize women are so much more than objects of pleasure, the frequency and need for sex decreases.

Monitor time spent on social media, TV channels, and explicit websites that promote sexual addictions. It is nothing but the work of Satan trying to take you down into the pit with no way out. Last but not least, seek counseling and rehab.

4. Develop A Prayer Life

Most people will say overcoming adversity is challenging without a prayer life. Did you know miracles happen when we set our hearts to prayer? Personal and group prayers are powerful. We are encouraged to keep going when we pray about our situations. Jesus prayed all the time; think about that. If he prayed to the Father, so can you and I.

CHAPTER ELEVEN
Extension of Gratitude

I am grateful that there were so many people spiritually sent to help me gain sobriety. There's one person in particular who pulled me out of the iron teeth of drug addiction during a low point in my life, and that was Dr. Sullivan.

Dr. Sullivan was an outstanding minister over the Harvey House Program, a church leader, and a friend who saw something in me that nobody else did. As a visionary, Dr. Sullivan helped me to be my best self. He saw the future Ray Banks, a new man coming forth.

One day, in a conversation, he said, "I like your story; it sounds good. I'm interested in what your story will be like in two years." He let me know then that there would be a complete recovery through his rehab program.

Dr. Sullivan reassured me everything would be fine, but I wasn't sure how it would turn out. I listened and learned anyway. I went to church frequently and did everything they asked me to do. I absorbed every sermon and Bible study meeting like a sponge. You could say I was on a mission.

If you let God do a new work for you, He will create a brand new you. See, God will send people to your rescue. Can you imagine being completely free of deadly drugs and crazy sexual fantasies, all of which stop you from being your most fabulous self? I know for a fact that God will take these things away. I recalled a scripture that says, *"Behold, I create new heavens and a new earth, and all former things shall not be remembered."* (Isaiah 65:17, KJV). I was becoming a new man.

Dr. Sullivan was a good Samaritan who took a guy like me, a drug addict living on the streets. I allowed myself to be robbed of everything. He saw the good in me, took me under his wings, and walked me through some of the most challenging days of my life, which was the pain of overcoming drug and sex addictions. Without Dr. Sullivan's guidance, I wouldn't be walking around today. I probably would be dead.

During those years of recovery, I received many invitations to dinners and conferences with Dr. Sullivan, his family, and church members. He had a generous spirit and freely gave to strangers. During the dinners, I observed how he quietly tipped the servers and waiters as they served our tables.

He taught me that a man should be a servant to his family, especially his wife. When I arrived for dinner at his home, I would find him cutting the meat at the table while his wife chatted with guests until Dr. Sullivan served dinner. He taught me that being a servant was a way to get to know your wife. It was a matter of honor. His service to his family taught me about service to my loved ones and, yes, to everyone.

He taught me that a wife takes care of her husband's needs, including cooking, cleaning, caring for their children, and so much more. Dr. Sullivan demonstrated that he honored his wife for her devotion to the family, which was an eye-opener for me. His way taught me how I should honor and respect my wife, and I did.

One day, I received a ministry house credit card to purchase cleaning items for the church. I took a few of the guys with me, and as I shopped, I noticed how they were quietly checking out the items I purchased for the church. At the same time, I bought items for myself, which I paid separately with my money, not with the ministry card. The brothers said, "Man, you gonna' put your stuff on the ministry card? I know if I had that card, I would." I turned to them and said: "Naw, man, I'm buying this stuff separately. I got my card, and I ain't trying to dishonor God."

Again, God will try us with honesty and dishonesty when you least think he won't. Anything done in the dark will soon come to light, which taught me about honesty and integrity. God always sees you when others are not looking. Your real character is when no one sees what you do. Only you and God know that part of you. I'm saying we dishonor God when we take what doesn't belong to us.

Dr. Sullivan was a wise man who taught me about integrity, something the streets don't do. Those young guys who left Harvey House will remember the wisdom and virtues taught by Dr. Sullivan. I now teach everything I learned from Dr. Sullivan and the leaders in the church to young men who receive the very same principles Dr. Sullivan and the church gave me.

Back in those days, as I studied with Dr. Sullivan and absorbed his teachings at Harvey House, God began to grant me the illustrious gifts of faith, sobriety, trust, ministry, service, giving, gratitude, honesty, integrity, an understanding of manhood, love for my wife and family, community, and perseverance. Not only did I receive those gifts, but I will carry them forever with me. All men under Dr. Sullivan's teachings received those same blessings. In 2017, Dr. Sullivan passed away. Thank you, Dr. Sullivan, for walking with me and molding me into the man I am today.

CHAPTER TWELVE
The Mission of Education

The New Millennium brought with it yet another new calling for me, one that I didn't see or understand. Two thousand and three brought many local elections, including the Thornton Township High School District 205 School Board Election.

Being a school board member was off my radar and something I didn't consider doing. All of that changed through the convincing of Dr. Sullivan. One evening in a board meeting, Dr. Sullivan insisted that I run as a board member for District 205. I thought he was joking. Becoming a board member for 205 was out of my reach, and in my opinion, board members acted stuck up, and being stuffy wasn't me.

Dr. Sullivan hadn't been wrong about the outcome of my life so far, so why would he be wrong about asking me to be on a ballot to become a school district board member?

I want to be perfectly honest. Something was bothering me about running for the board member seat. I didn't think I was smart enough to win. I thought of myself as a nobody coming from the west side of Chicago, running the streets non-stop and selling drugs. So, who would believe in me or trust me on some school board?

I agreed and prepared to run for the school board seat. I filled out all of the necessary papers to become a board member. We then canvassed the neighborhood to get signatures and handed out fliers throughout the school district's residential area. Dr. Sullivan told me nothing beats a failure but a try. After that, we set up a campaign office in my home.

As election day approached, we knocked on doors, and I introduced myself to many community members. I did everything I knew to do, and soon, the day of the election came around. I was nervous and unsure about the outcome of our work to win the election.

On the evening of election night, the Spirit of God Fellowship team and I went to the church to watch the election outcome. We looked at the votes and watched the school board numbers come in. There I was at the top, running ahead of the other candidates. I didn't know what I was doing and didn't think I was smart enough to win. However, I won the election and am still a board member of School District 205.

In my eyes, I came from nothing and didn't want to become anything until God delivered me from the shackles and bondage of drug use. I came to know and trust in God with my life. That is how I became a Restoration Youth Leader, Restoration Minister Executive Director, Vice-President of Restoration Ministries, and now, for over two decades, a Thornton High School District 205 board member.

One of my most significant achievements was initiating the District 205 Student Board of Education, which we started over 15 years ago. District 205 is the only Illinois school district with a student board of education, and for that, I am incredibly proud to be part of that initiative.

The students on the board of education, elected by their peers, are selected for their leadership abilities and outstanding academic excellence throughout high school. After graduating, these high school board members attend some of America's finest colleges and universities.

The idea of the high school board of education came from the youth program at our church, run by the junior board. Dr. Jerry Doss, Assistant Superintendent for School District 205, and Kamala Butler were instrumental in creating this program with me. Creating the student school board of education is one of my most significant accomplishments. For this, I owe gratitude to Dr. Sullivan's vision and to God, who blessed me with the ability to trust in him; even when I wasn't sure how things would turn out, I still walked through every process needed to get me where I am today.

In 2006, my son Freddie graduated from Thornwood High School, and before graduation, he received a scholarship to go to college to play football at Mercyhurst University in Erie, Pennsylvania.

Before his graduation that year, I served as Chaplain for Thornwood's football team. My job was to attend practice with the players, pray with them, and counsel them when needed. During this time, I also attended a four-day training camp in Michigan.

Today, my son is a coach at Colorado State, and many other men on the Thornwood football team have gone on to do great things. I share this with you because everything that happened to me happened for a reason. Like I said, I saw none of this in my future, but God and others did. I couldn't give up now because my family depended on me, and I had to rely on God and myself. The new man had fully manifested as Dr. Sullivan had said, and there was no thought of returning to my old ways and habits.

CHAPTER THIRTEEN
Deaneen

In 2015, I decided to join Blast Fitness Center in Dolton, Illinois. At the time, I weighed around 250 pounds. I took out an annual membership and started attending workouts at night, around 9 p.m. I suffered from high blood pressure and high cholesterol, and the much-needed exercise would help. The doctor told me I needed to lose weight, which motivated me to join the health club.

Around this time, I was still working for Restoration Ministries, clocking in from 9 a.m. to 6 p.m., which was a decent schedule. Later in the evening, I played basketball and went to the health club.

I took a vacation from the Restoration Ministry in December to do Christmas shopping. Around that time, I developed a routine of going to the health club. In the evenings, I would spend time shopping for the kids from 6 to 7 p.m., and then I would go to the fitness center for the rest of the evening.

During the Christmas season, one evening, I went to the health club and decided to walk around and casually wandered into the women's section of the fitness center. I watched them do some vigorous workouts for a while. I saw an aerobics instructor leading the class, and she was harsh on the ladies. As I stood there watching them keep up with the instructor, the female instructor approached me and said, "Are you going to join us?" I replied, "No, because I don't see any paramedics around here." She turned around and went back to instruct the class. I walked out of the room where the ladies were doing aerobics, headed to the men's area, and worked out.

Later that night, the aerobics instructor approached me at the health club, introduced herself, and told me her name was Deaneen. She first asked me why I hadn't joined the class. As I said, I told her I didn't see the paramedics around in case I needed them. I told her that she was dogging those girls. She kind of smiled at me, and then we began to talk.

Suddenly, a bold question rose in me. I told Deaneen, "I'm going to ask you something unusual." She said, "What?"

"Go out with me tonight," I asked her without hesitating. She looked at me straight in my eyes, crossed her arms, and half-smiled. I knew the answer that was coming, so I waited for it. She quickly shifted her weight, kept her arms crossed, and told me she had another aerobics class to instruct in a different workout facility.

To my surprise, before heading to the next class, Deaneen gave me her number, even though I didn't think I would get the number. I thought she would walk away, and that would be the end of our conversation.

I was still feeling the effects of the divorce between me and my second wife, Angela. I had split several years with my wife before meeting Deaneen, and I felt some way about how the marriage ended with Angela and me. I was married twice, and now I was in a place where I didn't want to be "tied up" in a marital situation. However, being a man, I was okay with having a relationship.

Before leaving home that evening, I prayed to God and said, "God, I don't want a woman; I'm just fine the way I am." What brought that on, I don't know. Meeting Deaneen at the health club was not expected, nor did I see it coming. A few hours prior, I had prayed to God and said I didn't want a woman, but again, my life was about to change for the better.

* * *

Three days later, I called Deaneen to see where her head was. When she answered, she told me she was at the health club instructing an aerobics class. She sounded out of breath, and l could tell she was busy. She couldn't talk long, so we hung up, and she promised to call me back later.

The next time we talked, Deaneen told me she was taking a fitness class to get a certificate in fitness training. She then explained that she needed a man and a woman to complete the course and asked if I could be her male test subject.

I told her I didn't have the money to pay for the class. She assured me that there was no fee and all I had to do was show up.

In the first meeting, we filled out a lot of paperwork about our health. As the barrage of questions continued, I peeped at the fact that the questions she asked me were not entirely about my health, but she was asking about me on a more personal level. "Hold up. I thought you were supposed to be talking about my health. Are you talking about me?" I asked her.

She broke down and said, "I kind of like you." I told her, "I like you too." From then on, we started communicating more by phone.

When I discovered we were 13 years apart, I initially hesitated to talk to Deaneen. I was much older than her, which didn't sit well with me. One day, I explained in a conversation that I didn't feel right talking to her since I was much older. "You're the only one concerned about my age, not me," she said.

Once we cleared the air about the age differences, she told me she was in the middle of a divorce and would soon finish it. I was concerned about her divorce since I was an advocate who tried to keep people's marriages together. I didn't know whether to step back until she finished the divorce or keep calling her. Everything worked out in our favor, and we continued to stay in touch.

As the old year ended, a new year began. I entered 2016 with the prospect of a new and budding relationship with Deaneen.

I never visited her home, nor did she come to mine. However, we continued to talk on the phone for hours. If we spoke at nine at night, it wouldn't be until 2:00 a.m. before the call ended. We discussed everything: childhood, relationships, divorce, people we knew, our dreams and goals. By then, I had developed a good relationship with Deaneen like no other I had previously.

We dated and went out for two years, and on November 11, 2018, we married at the Spirit of God Fellowship in the presence of 240 church members. We started planning our wedding with only about 50 people in attendance, and when we looked at the list, we saw 150 invitees, so we decided to keep the invitations private. We kept our money and put it on our honeymoon.

It was an unusual wedding because we didn't have an invitation list. We decided that the wedding was held right after church services, and everyone who came to the church attended the wedding. If members weren't in attendance during church services, they missed our wedding.

After we exchanged vows, we spent four days in Fort Lauderdale and boarded a 7-day cruise to the beautiful island of the Bahamas. Our cruise was everything we had hoped it to be and more. The Bahamas welcomed us with open arms, which was well worth the money.

Fort Lauderdale is a central cruise port to the Bahamas, Jamaica, Mexico, Grand Cayman Island, Cozumel, and St. Maarten.

By now, my life had come full circle. I had a new wife and a family home and spent valuable time with my children. As Dr. Sullivan once said, "I like your story, but it is the future that I am truly interested in."

What was it about my life that Dr. Sullivan knew that was completely oblivious to me? Everything he predicted had come to pass, and still, the new man within me continued to evolve well into the new millennium. I had long disassociated myself from my former life, and at every opportunity I came across, I ministered to those struggling with drugs, letting them know that if God could change my life, he could change theirs.

My marriage was going well. The youth ministries were moving positively, and all I managed were thriving. I was doing good, and it all seemed like a dream.

In 2020, after two years of marriage, I had a stroke. I was preparing for an online teaching course for the Spirit of God Fellowship Church one morning. All of a sudden, my body felt strange. I couldn't raise my arms or legs or couldn't walk. I didn't know what was going on, and they rushed me to Shirley Ryan's Ability Lab, where I stayed for 30 days.

The stroke left me paralyzed, and during recovery, I was in a wheelchair. I wasn't able to talk because I had what was called Aphasia. Whatever I processed in my mind, I couldn't articulate it, and this became very frustrating, but I had to develop a deeper faith in God to get me through my ordeal.

My wife became my interpreter. She would tell me what people were saying, and in return, she would tell people what I was saying.

In the months ahead, I would undergo many procedures and tests. I also saw a speech pathologist and occupational therapist weekly to strengthen my muscles.

The doctors told me they would get me back on track. I knew they had to, and with my trust and faith in God, they did.

After being released from the hospital, I attended the Shirley Ryan's Rehabilitation Outpatient Center for therapy for five days a week from July to November 2020. This happened when COVID-19 began to peak.

As I lay on my bed one morning and still couldn't speak, God spoke to me and said, *"My son, you will speak for me again."* No kidding. The words I heard made me think I was going crazy. Here I am, unable to speak or move. Because of my condition, I thought it would be physically impossible to talk. That message of: *"My son, you will speak for me again"* kept coming back to me, and not too many months later, my speech returned. Being able to talk again was a slow, gradual process. With the help of a speech therapist, I could speak again.

The daily occupational therapy at Shirley Ryan Rehab was a tremendous help, even though, for months, I had to get around with the help of a wheelchair. During one visit to the rehab center, I recalled the doctor saying, "On your next visit, don't come in a wheelchair." That was excellent news to hear. I started using a cane to walk, and that was significant progress for what I had gone through. Also, during that time, as a stroke patient, I participated in studies, which was a great help to improve me. The Spirit of God Fellowship Church asked me to speak again, and to this day, I am still teaching there.

God made his healing power real in my life, and I noticed how the words I wanted to speak became more manageable and clearer.

For 30 years, I ministered to guys on drugs. I ran into many rough patches, and I came through every last one of them. God had to be with me through all of this, too. He didn't bring me that far to drop me. As I continued to heal,

I hung onto God's word: *"My son, you will speak again,"* and I did.

Today is Wednesday, January 15, 2024, and I speak and walk without the assistance of a cane. I can raise both hands to my head and do anything a normal person can do. It's not all over for God when you think it's over because He will make a way out of no way. God is good!

EPILOGUE
The Footsteps of A Trailblazer

All children are a blessing to their families, which is mine. A child's calling can be fulfilled in this lifetime under the anointing of their parents' ministry, and sometimes it's not. Placing your footprints in this life for your children to follow is a mighty task only God can anoint and sanction. During the early years of my fatherhood, being an example for my children was not what I was about at all. I was more into what led me to do what I did, and I never dreamed that things would later turn in my favor and my children's favor. Much of my life and how I was living my life went in the wrong direction, and my children witnessed a good deal of it, something I'm certainly not proud of. On the canvas of my life, I painted a picture of my life that was not so beautiful so my children could make a clear choice. The option for them to choose wisely stood before them. All I wanted for them was to make better choices than what I had made.

At first glance, we never see the reason or the rhyme of our lives, why we do what we do. If we are lucky, we wake up and desire a need for change. Thank God, my eyes came open!

Change will come when we fully accept God's word, no matter how challenging. We must meditate on this change and make it a reality daily.

What I went through with drugs, many people do not make it through, and that's the truth. It is not always an easy transition to return to a typical day-to-day life when all you know is using drugs. It was a profound spiritual transformation that got me through. My life was an open book in many ways. My children saw and knew things about me that will stay with them forever. God is my judge, and I don't have a heaven or hell to put no one in and vice-versa.

I am so happy that God led my children. Some followed me in my church ministry programs, while others pursued God-blessed careers.

Charla is my oldest daughter, who graduated from Thornridge in 1998. She is the eldest of the sisters in the family. Charla will tell the family many stories about my transformation and what it took for me to be delivered.

In 1996, when my family lived in Harvey, Monique, my adoptive daughter, and my kids' cousin came to live with us during her junior high years. She transferred from Thornton to Thornwood High School, where she excelled in Speech. Both high schools she attended are part of three public state schools that serve the student body, grades 9th-12th grade of School District 205. In 2001, Monique graduated from Thornwood. In 2019, she became a speech coach for Thornwood. Today, Monique advocates for the homeless community.

My daughter, Racheal, was a member of The Spirit of God Fellowship Praise Dance. She, too, graduated from Thornwood High in 2003.

My daughter Pamela has been the Restoration Ministries Youth Program Manager since 2014. She worked during the earlier years of the restoration ministries program when I first became a pastor.

Danielle was another adoptive daughter of mine born and raised on Chicago's west side. Danielle would visit my home during the summer months and would return to the west side to return to school. She came to live with us when she was 16 up until her late twenties. Due to Danielle's heartbreaking, tragic death in December 2023, she passed away at the age of 29.

I thank my daughters, including my beloved son, Freddie, who is now an educated, professional college football coach, for allowing me to be their father. They grew up to be beautiful in the eyes of the Lord, and I see their beauty as well. My life is a journey of endurance, gratitude, and faith for all of us, and I am so glad each of you was there for me, as I will always be here for all of you. God, Faith, You, and Deaneen are the parts that anchor my life. *To God be the glory for what he has done for me and my beloved family*!

ABOUT THE AUTHOR

Ray Banks is the author of the *Ray Banks Story: A Testimony of God's Restoration Power*. Born and raised on Chicago's westside, Mr. Banks is a pastor and youth minister advocate in the Chicago Southland. For 35 years, under the Restoration Ministry, he served as Restoration Youth Leader, Restoration Minister Executive Director, and Vice-President of Restoration Ministries. He serves as a school board member for Thornton Township High School District 205. Mr. Banks is married to Mrs. Deaneen Merritt-Banks. For more information about Restoration Ministries, please contact Mr. Ray Banks at (708) 217-1048.

Made in USA - Kendallville, IN
41909_9781681115955
08.26.2025 2057